AF447724

A Ten Or Twenty Pence
Poems Imprint

Quiet Darkness Poems
Love After Love

Christopher Sanderson
A Coastmoor Publication

Contents

These poems, and this book, began life as the outcome of my morning meditations, indeed the book was in my meditation room for quite some time so as to not risk losing the inspirations.

But then an afternoon of songwriting came along, and the notebook had to be used for verse, chorus, pre-chorus, post chorus and bridge.

In the exercise I was told that the first line must be the truth. This stopped me in my tracks, fortunately my co-writer explained that it should at the very least sound like the truth.

The poems, at least in terms of the meditation reference, then lost there way a little as other poets, and biscuits, and cafés all tried to introduce their influence.

Fortunately my candle lit space, and the great outdoors came together to help me finish a collection, which I hope shares some of the joy which it gifted to me.

Christopher
2022

One Way In
There May Be Many Others

It is a different kind of thing
A love out of nowhere
Other than from the meditations
Of the morning

What is it that I wish to achieve
What wishes might I reach for
How might I discover the truth
The truth of that which I am seeking

Not now knowing where to start
Or what the out-turns may be
Misunderstanding how this works
Or where and how to find the clarity

All That I Am

I am nothing more
Than mind, body
Soul, eros, and spirit

Which
Through memories, observations, and dreams
Gift me feelings, thoughts, and ideas

Opportunities that allow me
To plot a way forwards, and sideways
Through this singular journey of my one life

Disappointment

I dislike intellectuals, mostly
Because I am not in their gang
But also because I believe they stole
That which I thought belonged to me

Back again
In the domain of intellectuals
Who have once more refused me
Entrance to join their ranks

This time though there is hope
As I walk past several Francis Bacon originals
Also a Giacometti
Whose standing woman appears to lean

Unlike the Healing Man Buddha
Who silently promises
To make well
All in my world and its surroundings

Light Years Away

So not too too bad
Not to have been admitted
To the inner sanctum
Of the society of thieves

Thirty-seven years ago
This past summer
Take care to check the date
You know how my memory is

If I turn to sculpture
Will it be
To learn the inside out
Of the rest of my mind

Particularly to practice
That return from infinity
Where surely, at least once
I am bound to have travelled

Misplaced Steps

The biscuit box is empty
The *Home Body* poems are read
At least today's consignment

For my father was also a wagon driver
Delivering concrete pavement edges
To the navvies laying new roads

In this way I empathise, sympathise
With the poet Rupi Kaur
Yet I feel there is distance between us

Which makes the point, to me at any rate
That nothing changes, which you may recognise
As a David Bowie album, from back in the day

I don't have a lot more to say
That album includes *Let's Dance*
And we did dance, in one of my stories

Ash In Tow

The Bay hunkers down
As the wind introduces itself
To a day of majestical purpose

The wood-burner flue warms up
Even with the flames
Struggling to catch hold

What was that word
Which you failed to remember
After yesterday morning's meditation

Something similar in sound or meaning
To bestow or all aglow
Definitely with a resounding so so ending

Vacate
With Such Joy

I haven't got going
It's cold, I'm cold
I nearly bought a present
I almost sent a message
I felt, I felt
A bit better about myself

I haven't got going
The feeling is cold
The intention is colder
I did have one warm thought
Then another, about the icicles
At Hambleton, near Rutland Water

No, Not That Way

Instead of losing your attachments
Why not try to hold onto them
Try as hard as ever you can
Don't let go, whatever you do

Not of lost love
Or past memories
Not of secrets, or promises
Or anything which gifts you joy

It is foolish to believe
That if you lose attachments
You will relieve your suffering
If anything the opposite is so

Instead of banishment
Turn to celebration
Dust off the cobwebs from your photographs
Buy no more love-psychology books

Make a collage of words and pictures
To breathe new life
Into that which the miserable buggers
Would have you throw away

Disruptive
At Your Pleasure

So many thoughts
Way too many thoughts
Who is man enough
To hold onto so so many thoughts

Then the noises
Here, there, and everywhere the noises
Now, then, and whenever the noises
Up, down, and turnaround to the noises

But also
The glimpses of beauty
The deep releases of sneezes
To blow everything up, or close everything down

So many thoughts
The temples are vibrating
First with one thing, then with the other
Before it all kicks off all over again

Then the noises; where are you now
Where will you be tomorrow
Is there any chance at all
That we could share a conversation

Perceptive

Does the blackbird scuttle
Due to the sounds or the vibrations issued
By my feet heavily stepping on the flagstones

Or do my piercing eyes
Effectively order the bird to take cover
Beneath the winter bushes
Which are distinctly smothered in morning dew

Do you perceive more than I
Is there a morphic resonance
Which connects, outside of chance
Or coincidence; or am I simply lost

Is the date of the video being loaded
Any more significant than that of a birthday
Of course the experiments could be fake
But an academic taboo restricts disclosure

Instead to see you at the seashore
Where your consciousness expands
Out into a life within my life
A place where I am happy to welcome you

Déjà

As the estate grounds open up
I swallow thirty years
In the one gulp of northern air

In that one moment
Even in the previous moment
I was left elsewhere

And in that otherwise
Of *Poetry Otherwise*
I was becalmed by beauty

Never really knowing
If that is what knowing is
Of theatre under moonlight

And in that sea swell
Of waveless nights
With painters at the ready

In that event
Even in the previous event
I am curiously left without any doubts

Cuban Cigar

I do not have the energy
Or the desire
Or the effective concentration
To set about typing up

Rather to dwell
In the loss of self control
Caught up in the devilment
Of doing nothing at all

That is other than feeling
Sorry for myself
Coming over all melancholic
With the story left in the wings

Where he sings the songs of loss
Has his joss sticks at the ready
As the unsteadiness settles
And the butterflies land on dust

Rust covered energies abound
To the sounds of plucked guitars
And slow-puffed cigars, in the urban
Surroundings of yesterday's moon

One Line

In the bright sun of January
(So you know the time of year)
Yes in the warmth, at the breakfast table
(So you know the place, and the time of day)

Outside a strong Northerly breeze
(So you know which way the wind blows)
Also outside, a dog barks; this irritates me
(So you know that I do have irritations)

However the blue sky soaks up my annoyance
(And now you know that I like blue skies)

Nature
Returns To Music

Sky blue skies

Red brick houses

What are those berries

On the branches

Poking through

The green leaf bushes

It is too cold to walk

What, in these ice-grey skies

Why to set foot out

Better surely

To take to the couch

And listen

To *Spiegel im Spiegel*

Two Together

I have to consult another
About my writing
About my walking
About my searching the internet

And who might that other be
Could we be put in the know
Could we be trusted with your secret
Could you not tell us so

In the oasis of calm
As if a peaceful meditation
Of mind like sky
Perhaps as todays skies full of emptiness

I could tell
But who would that help
Not anyone that I know
And that's for sure

Yet, for the sake
Of the colloquial among you
I could talk of transference
And passionate island living

Cast Iron Range

Smokestacks and rampant flags
A winter's day like any other
Remember your mother
How peacefully she passed
How contented her later days

Will that happen for you
Are you about to turn
Impatience into contentment
Can you make your fire burn

In such and such
And all those other ways

Well Observed

Many Stories Told

Eventually the snow falls
Snow and light rain combine
My first time
With time to simply sit and watch

Yet soon, as if my observation
Was not called for
Both snow and rain decline
As the light fades

And, as the sky darkens
The time available shortens
Time for what, do I hear you ask
As I question that thought myself

Maybe doing nothing
Could be as good a place as any to start
And then perhaps to grow, incrementally
Until we reach doing everything

Maybe by now you too
Are thinking about Jules Verne
All of those fabulous Phileas Fogg adventures
As he went *Around the world in eighty days*

Galvanised Tin

It's slow time on a Sunday
With the way too hot
Black Americano

The old doorway is bricked up
But I don't give a jot
For the distressed style

And the open tray work
Leading to surface-mounted conduit
Reminds me too too much of my youth

Dust naturally gathers
On the chain suspended Bose speakers
Music, like me, hanging by a thread

Mindful
Joyful

On this day you passed away
You, Thich Nhat Hahn
My second grandfather

Called
In your 95th year
A new end to your meditations

Calm, Ease, Smile, Breathe
Present moment
Beautiful moment

Breath
Breathe in
Breath, breathe out

First Day Induction

Final Day Ceremony

The day of the novice
With a new life
Of dedication ahead

How to take this step
To enter into another family
What to leave behind

Stood on the wooden floor
Listening to the sound of the meditation bell
Watching the cremation's wood burning

Thinking of love
Of all the love known
Of all the love gifted and given

How to take the next step
To find a new mind for memory
To visualise a subtle sublime emptiness

Stood on the mother earth
Listening to the breath
The in-breath and the out-breath

Thinking of love
Of all of the loving kindness
On this day, and the coming days ahead

Impatient

Even today
I have continued the habit
Of starting the next task
Before finishing the last

I hadn't completed the poetry
When I decided to go into town
I had not typed up the darkness
When I thought to chase the light

Also, I didn't pack the iPhone
Into my shoulder bag
So these past four thousand steps
Will not be counted

But hey ho
The caramel waffles
Settled the score
Before the match had even started

It Ain't Heavy
It's My Computer

Don't follow the conversation
Return to your own thoughts
Don't listen to the singer
Write out your own lyrics

Don't look at the bald man
Typing on his laptop
Think of your own programmes
On the luggable Mac

Yes, cast. back to the graphs
Which you thought told the story
Think of the colour wheel
Where you believed in contrasting colours

Do not focus on the small memory
Or your complete data wipe-out
Think that you too can stroke
Your overgrown facial hair

Final Tenancy

For The Pub Landlord's Son

How light is the day
Without a trouble to care for
How far is the sight
From there to the seashore

How human the slight
When choosing the decor
How high flies the kite
When we opened the *White Door*

How the aircraft offered delight
To follow the marks on the cabin floor
No more panic, or freeze, or fight, or flight
Nothing stored away as then with the rip-roar

Let It Be Said

I have not found the straightjacket of form
I have been unable to adorn the monks gowns
My mind and body are free-formed from strata
And yes there are regrets, would I not
Wish to wear the emperor's new clothes
For I am nothing, and I will be nothing
And in between the water will only ripple slightly

All of these places which you engagingly talk of
They are not my places
I have no allegory or metaphor at hand
For you to hang your hat or your story on
I am a been there and done that sort of guy
What I write is what is real, and, for the sake
Of understanding I will leave it at that

Except of course for love, or companionship
For I have known these doubtful imposters
And worked out how to treat them the same
Although it is a secret, of secrets purpose
That is to say you must work it out
For no clues are to be found on this page
And the pencil marks will only serve to mislead

What We Forget

Where are your parents today
How old are you
Do you ask yourself these questions
As you place your offering at the altar
What have you learnt
From the teacher's profound teachings
I saw you thoughtful
I saw you joyful
I saw you, and now I don't
If I reach out
For someone other
Or some thing other
Am I
By necessity
Leaving the past behind

Psychology
A Personal Thing

The blue, black, and silver sky
A place for all offerings
All of light is beneath here
Except that illumination above

So there we have it
Out of my dark meditation room
Into the rest of the morning
Where words wait to be joined together

Meanwhile, here in the café
Mother's talk of daughter's depression
So right here, as well as in Tokyo
The black dog is present

Psychology

And, as these stranger's voices
Turn into fleeting whispers
Exchanging fears and experiences
This is the way support is shared

Also, advice is offered
For the daughter to get as far away as she can
From that boyfriend, who they have decided
Is a controlling, loathsome, individual

I know that she will be alright
Deep down I know that
But its been good to talk with you
What about your girl

Artist

On the cusp
Or the saddle
Where certainty
And uncertainty prevail

The small diamond
As head
The large diamond
As body

The narrow diamond
As hips
Thighs, knees
And feet

The whole thing
Then to be you
Sparkling, shiny
And beyond betrayal

Treasures
Of The Moments

A lack
Of love
Of self
Of confidence
Of interrogation
Or explanation

A need
To wait
To pause
To delay
To become more
Or less assured

A departure
Heavy eyelids
Dry mouth
A longer view
Ever so slightly
Out of focus

Gifts

And Recriminations

What you took
Is nothing near
What you have

But you did take
The whole damned lot
Left not an ounce of love

What you shook
Is nothing near
That closest shave

But you did shave
The whole damned lot
Left not a sign of stubble

What you look at
Is nothing near
The book you read

But you did read
The whole damned lot
Left not a word out of sorts

Playing

There is a flat platform
A flagged square
Or rectangle

This could be the starting point

There is a gradual slope
Lawn and flower bed
To a tall tree in the corner

This is the body of the story

Beyond the conifer
And over thee low wooden fence
Is the track, unmade and uneven

This has to be the way out

Storytelling

One man's life
Told as the story of a river
An unfolding continuum of one page sketches
One for each year of his life
But beginning in mid-life
The story told backwards and forwards

One man's life
Lets me settle
Into one man's life
Then the postman knocks on the door
To deliver the story
Of another man's life
Homeless, with mental issues

One man's life
This man
In care
Except that, yes
It could all disappear
In a line on a page
Or thanks to a disadvantaged mother

Festival

If this isn't the time
When would be ok
If I wasn't to give a sign
What would you have me say

And so we begin
Floating through the water reeds
Same as it ever was is our sin
Turning time back to misspent deeds

If that wasn't the case
What would be the truth
If I hadn't joined the race
Would I be here and not aloof

And so we end
Walking on the open moors
Same as it ever was is to lend
The season to our universal cures

Kumbh Mela
Albert Falzon

Straight ahead
With the energy
Of one man's punt

Drifting along
With the guidance
Of one man's oar

Embracing peace
Beneath the canopy
Of cotton and reed

Among a community
With a strength of purpose
To feed the soul

On a voyage
Along the holy river
Within his ambient sounds

Pause Button

In another place
Which for these few moments
Becomes my space

So much so
That I unbutton
My overcoat

And wait
For the words to flow
As I listen to other people's stories

Let The Good Times Roll

Tuck into the shortbread
With caramel and chocolate toppings
Knowing full well
That this is bad for you
But also good for you

The child, sat in the child's chair
Turns around, looks around
The taps his hands on the table
Much to the delight of his mother
His auntie, and his adoring grandma

This is the day
That he takes his first taste
On the path to sugar diabetes
Type I or type II who knows
But always supported by his family

Day Out
To The Old Places

Beside the canal
By the empty reservoir
At the entrance to the tunnel
In the spring sunshine
Of one more leap year

What kind of town is this
What kind of town is the other
Either way
They are both a long way away
And that's a fact

But then again
Not many places can be nearby
If as you say that the sea
Is one half of nearby
To your home locale

Whereas before
On the spine of the country
Where moorland, and peat, and bog
Happily co-exist, in more or less
Equal measure, to the rain

Racket

Tinnitus

Or stereo soundscapes

Which or which

Let's you know

That life is still with you

And that sloping roof

Beyond the hedgerows

Why and why

Is it at a right angle

To my window

Piano

And or violin

Out of both speakers

As I ponder

And deliberate

That such a voice

Can take me back

To such poor decisions

In the long

And distant past

Tricks

Of Disappearance

I write to no one
The fountain flows no more
Yet
There is a lightness
An emptiness
Beginning to dance

I write to any one
Even those
Who are not here
Yet whose spirit
Flows in and out
Of all of my minds

Behold
Hold Steady

The candle lights the room
A small room, with no windows
This is a safe place
My safest place

We wanted
To share our bodies
I wanted yours
You wanted mine

But the world was not ready
For our connection
For our collision
For our night under the stars

The fade
Begins to fade
The excitement
Calms to a storm for no one

Gold Dust

This is not about love
I have already been too careless with that
This is about being free
To be alone with the loneliness

Also about waste
To have wasted three score year and ten
To end up nowhere, with next to nothing
Except the buckets full of memories

Catching On

A collar
A heel
The need to feel
Somehow really good

A gesture
A pleasantness
The need to suggest
A sense of a new beginning

A hand
A smile
The need to style
Our very next moves

A morning sun
A flowing breeze
The need to seize
This beautiful day

Meditation

There need be no one else
In this time of stillness
To be honest it's better that way

For peace and quiet
Is a prerequisite
To find and enter the deeper thoughts

Just now for instance
Taken to the meadow
Taken to the island seas

And before that
To nowhere at all
Looking into the near and far distance

Departures

I was searching
I found love
I am leaving

It is a dull day
The hedge tops have been trimmed
Although further south they haven't

There are blue skies
At this point of the compass
The sea sparkles to move me

I am searching
I found love
I am leaving

Before The Voice

I will have this moment
Nothing can take that away
And so it is also with zillions
Of previous memories

But this particular time
Of decision and indecision
Need to find its own secure place
On the see-saw of life

That is why I mention
The Victoria Sponge
And cup of Americano coffee
As I look out over marsh and sea

I thought it was my friend the farmer
With a walkie-talkie
Looking for the Red Kite
But I could have been mistaken

Slide

The rains have been
The sea has been
The salt flats are soddened

The ground slips
Beneath my fanciful trainers
I do a kind of arthritic splits

The style stays with me
One more accident
In a lifetime full of calamities

Stabilisation
Reclamation

I could be anywhere
But happen to be here
Trying my best to fall over

Listen to the waves
Listen to the wind
Listen to the curlew or plover

Taking a photograph
Of reeds and grasses
Flattened by the flood waters

Hardly A Ripple

In this aloneness

There are no leaders to follow

No instructions to misunderstand

I can go my own way

Even if I stumble

And yes, sometimes fall

The moorhen

Plunges half of her body

Headfirst, into the black water

Out Of Space

I declare

You are my meteor star

Curving through the curved air

Of a deeper love

Steeper than the steepest mountain

A fountain of youth and truth and beauty

So light, so happy

On a blue sky Saturday

Such a tight feeling

That says love stay with me

The keeper of the song

All in all another beautiful day

Sugar

Was it the dessert pastilles
Which lifted my mood
Or was it my morning meditation
Which set me in good stead
For the rest of this beautiful day

Was it the café
Here, there, or anywhere
Which set the seal
On the deal of love
About to be offered

Strines
Clearance

This isn't my moor
But it is my ringing in the ears
My vibrations of being almost at home
Yet a long way from love

Thinking it must be an external sound
I open the car door
To hear nothing but the sheep
And the sound of scrub smoke slowly rising

Brown, and green, and purple
Yes, yes, oh boy yes I'll bless my love
For the purple heather
The brown, green, and beautiful purple heather

Test Says No

And so for the not so well their bids are due

But

You pushed on, you pushed out

Now

Your friends, and family are also not well

Yet

They also push on, push out

This way

The bugs spread at quite a rate

Until

In effect

We no longer catch it

Instead it visits us

In our alone and lonely quarters

Quarantined from the world

To such an extent

That we too wonder

If we could work on-line

But

Doing what, what can we do

Even with

The virus for our inspiration

Gardening Leave

Outdoors

In March

In recovery mode

Still wheezing

Though slightly less of a cough

The pebbles

Are haphazard

And ragged

With grass growing through

Even in the shingle

It all seems less than imperfect

Although more beautiful

With the strong spring sun

And the clear blue skies

Even the jets, overhead, have a good rhythm

Sublime

Nature is beauty
And that's for sure
Yet man
With his miraculous jet engine
Which I was taught about
Indeed went on a school trip to see
As a teenage lad over fifty years ago
May be a worthwhile rival

At the moment thought
To hear the noisy rattle and clatter
Of the recycle bin being wheeled back to base
Alongside my garden hedge
Makes me realise
That progress can be slow, if at all
Especially when ordinary men
And municipal councils are involved

About Turn

This is no anniversary
Except it is my first day
Back in meditation
Oh yes, and the sun shines
In through my window

This then is the celebration
A time of presence
Formed by the muse of joy
As only morning sunlight
Is able to offer

Yesterday I read Tolstoy
As he talked of art
Of beauty, of love
Though not in an empowering way
Rather to dispute what others have said

I myself find
That art and love and beauty
Let alone nature
Fill my life with such wonder
That they offer a path to understanding

Sublime

If ever we should doubt
The need to plot that course
To the promise of the promised land

If ever we should find out
About the judgements of The Bourse
Or of those groups which society banned

Step into the mud
Of the salt marsh
Or the estuary

Feel your feet sink
Your heart also
For what has slipped away

The wind, and sun
Will bring life
Where you thought love had perished

The night, the day
Both will replenish
And for that we can be grateful